Bun Eats the Herbs

By Sally Cowan

Pip and Bun played
in the yard.

Pip hid in a clump of ferns.

But his fluffy tail stuck out!

Bun jerked Pip's tail!

Then she dashed off and hid.

Bun hid by the old gate.

She stuck her head
into a hole.

She could smell herbs!

Sniff, sniff!

Bun dug with her feet.

She squished into the hole!

Bun popped out into
Miss Pang's yard.

She could see a big bed
of herbs.

Bun had a quick bite.

The herbs were **so** good!

She ate some more ...

Chomp, chomp, chomp!

Tam could see Pip stuck
in the hole.

She had to jerk him out!

"Dad," yelled Tam.
"Bun got out!"

They rushed into
Miss Pang's yard.

She looked stern.

"My herbs!" she yelled.
"The nerve of this bunny!"

Dad and Tam drove
to the plant shop.

They got lots of herb pots.

Tam waited at the kerb for Dad.

Dad blocked up the hole.

Tam gave Miss Pang
the herb pots.

Then Tam and Dad planted
the herbs for Miss Pang.

Miss Pang had a big smile.

Tam got a pot of herbs, too.

She served a leaf to Bun and Pip.

Bun and Pip were happy.

CHECKING FOR MEANING

1. Whose herbs does Bun eat? *(Literal)*

2. What are some of the herbs Bun tries? *(Literal)*

3. How would you describe Miss Pang throughout the story? *(Inferential)*

EXTENDING VOCABULARY

clump	What is a *clump* in the story? What else might you find in a clump?
jerked	What does the word *jerked* mean? What other word could have been used when Bun jerked Pip's tail?
nerve	What does Miss Pang mean when she yells, *"The nerve of this bunny!"*? What other meanings does the word *nerve* have?

MOVING BEYOND THE TEXT

1. Have you tried dill or mint? Did you like them?

2. Where is a good hiding spot in the schoolyard or your garden?

3. What other things do people grow in their gardens?

4. What does it take to be a good gardener?

SPEED SOUNDS

ar	er	ir	ur	or

PRACTICE WORDS

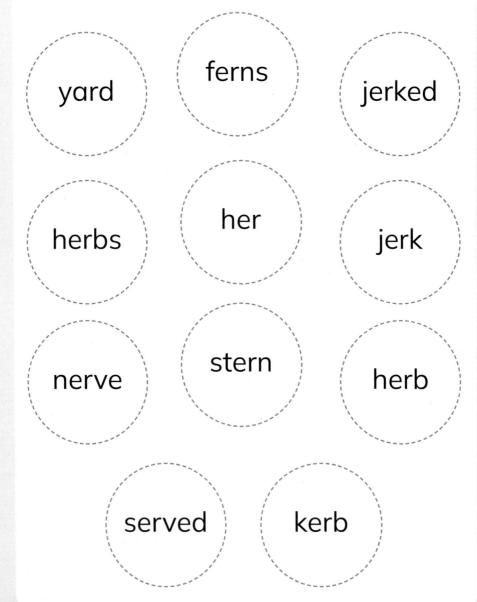

yard

ferns

jerked

herbs

her

jerk

nerve

stern

herb

served

kerb